Mummy's Little Helper

Mummy's Little Helper

by

Sarah Davies

Insight Into Action

Copyright © Sarah Davies 2009
First published in 2009 by Insight into Action (IIA)
15 Keswick Road, Bournemouth, BH5 1LP
Revised edition 2014

Distributed by Lightning Source

British Library Cataloguing in Publication Data
A catalogue record for this book is available from the
British Library

ISBN 978-0-9561444-2-3

Typeset by Amolibros, Milverton, Somerset
This book production has been managed by Amolibros
Printed and bound by Lightning Source

With love and thanks to Jonathan and Laura
To Sally and Anne
And to all my clients over the years
Who have taught me so much.

contents

One   1

Two   4

What babies and children really need   5

The power of projection   14

Three   17

The concept of inner child   17

Four   19

How to heal the inner child   19

Appendix One   31

Step 1   Validation   31

Step 2   Love   31

Step 3   Re-education   32

Appendix Two   33

Examples   34

A   Male, late twenties, low self-esteem   34

B   Female, early forties. Relationship difficulties.   36

C   Male, fifties. Depression.   38

D   Female, early twenties. Career guidance.   39

E   Female, late thirties. Lack of relationship.   42

F   Female, forties. Anxiety.   43

G   Female, fifties. 'Lonely' and ill.   45

H   Male, late thirties. Concerned about his drinking. 46

I   Female, late twenties. Anxiety.   48

J   Female, seventies. 'Unhappy'.   49

one

Are you familiar with an aching, inner emptiness that is never satisfied; a huge black hole lurking just beneath the surface that in your lowest moments will suck you down into a bottomless pit of despair; a hole that you do your best to fill with food, alcohol, drugs, sex? Do you have a habit of flitting from one relationship to another, constantly searching for love? Or is shopping your addiction of choice? Perhaps you have perfected the art of escapism and keep so busy that you succeed in distracting yourself from the recognition of this vast, gnawing pain at the core of your being. It is perfectly possible to ignore it or to deny totally its existence. Many people do. But only for a while because its denial exacts a hefty price; anything within our psyche which we choose to bury does not go away; it lies in wait for an opportune moment to reappear, eventually, with continued denial, wreaking its revenge on emotional and physical health.

If this inner emptiness rules your life, consciously or unconsciously, then you have lost your 'real' self. This real self is the person you had the potential to become, had you been allowed and encouraged to acknowledge and express what you were feeling as a child. In other words, had you been truly respected. Life, in the shape of parents with all their flaws, and society, with its frequent lack of true valuing of children, has eaten away at this potential until you are left as only a fraction of that which you might have become. This leaves a hollow inside and a brittle, coping, outer self which we present to the world to persuade ourselves and others that we are 'all right'. It fools most people most of the time because so many others are doing the same thing.

No doubt there are many possible causes but my work as a therapist over many years has shown me the prevalence of this problem and has led me on a search, first to find out why it is happening and secondly to find a simple, practical answer to help heal myself, my children and my clients.

No book can be a substitute for a really good therapist. I exclude from that category someone who only enables you to reach an intellectual understanding of your difficulties. For some, that may be enough. For me, that is not resolution. Thinking and feeling are different realms and not interchangeable. An emotional problem requires an emotional solution and that is what this book is about. I also exclude those therapists who, in any way, encourage the perpetuation of a victim mentality. Sitting in a heap feeling sorry for yourself is inexcusable. So is blame. Face the fact that you are never going to get from your parents something they are incapable of giving: even if they are still alive and, in the best of all possible circumstances, willing to do their own inner work, nobody but you can heal your emotional pain and it is no one else's responsibility. Despite this, we fall into the trap of thinking that if only we could meet the right partner, they would heal us and all would be well. Not so; we take into our adult relationships all our unresolved childhood issues. You were born with your particular lessons to learn, and your parents and life experiences are the necessary means of that learning. This is your problem, your challenge, your learning experience. Embrace it.

This book will show you how.

two

 What I discovered led me to believe that the cause might lie in our often inadequate parenting skills. Nobody teaches us how to be parents. We learn by example from our own parents or caretakers and do either what was done to us or, if we were very unhappy, try to do it differently and end up over-compensating.

Thank goodness parents are not perfect: were they so, their behaviour would be poor preparation for meeting the difficulties and challenges of life. Even with the best of intentions, parents make mistakes and, regretfully, some lack those good intentions. That does not mean that they set out to deliberately harm their child but rather that children may be regarded as an accessory or an inconvenience; something that detracts from the parents' own perceived needs. It is common to suppose that a child's requirements are the simple, practical things of life; food, warmth and clothes.

Parents work hard in order to provide those necessities. Frequently, they work even harder to provide the other material and materialistic desires of their offspring. Busy parents may justify their busyness by claiming they are 'doing it for the children', whilst others, unable to tell their children that they love them, buy gifts instead. Things become a substitute. But a substitute for what?

What babies and children really need

Although I use the term 'mother' throughout, obviously this is interchangeable with anyone in a caretaker role.

An ideal mother will instinctively 'mirror' her baby. You will see her copying and reflecting back to her baby his or her facial expressions. This is the fundamental key to the child's present and future emotional wellbeing for it says "I know what you are feeling and it is all right to feel it." This is easily done when the baby is smiling but what usually happens when the baby cries? If the mother is tired, depressed or busy she may choose, for a while, to ignore her baby's crying. More often, unable to tolerate the noise and desperately wanting to make it right for her baby, she will immediately pick up the infant, making suitably soothing noises as she does so. This omits the vital step of acknowledgment and validation, the "I know what you are feeling and it is all right to feel it"; in fact, her action is coming more from her need than that of her baby. This step cannot be overemphasised for there is a world of difference between the mother satisfying her baby's needs before her own or unconsciously prioritising her own needs for recognition and mirroring. So, ideally, if the baby is crying, the mother will make that same crying face to the baby who quickly recognises what the mother is doing –acknowledging and validating its emotions. Only then will she smile and reassure.

When a small child is accustomed to this behaviour on the part of its mother, it grows into adulthood with a strong sense of safety, security and sense of self.

One of the consequences of ignorance or ignoring this step is that the baby grows up habitually putting others' needs before its own. That, in theory, may sound good and unselfish. But here we are talking about an unconscious pattern of behaviour that is unhealthily hooked into actively getting other people's needs met for them: so much so that this individual will feel profoundly uncomfortable and unsafe were their own needs to be met, and therefore will go out of their way to avoid that happening. Because a baby's physical survival depends on the adult, the baby learns to adapt its behaviour in order to be pleasing to the mother, thereby ensuring its survival. As a baby, this person develops antennae to pick up and interpret its mother's mood. Were you to see this in action, you would notice the baby's eyes following its mother wherever she goes. This effectively provides the mother with what she is missing and missed out on when she herself was a baby – mirroring. The mother is looking to her baby for what her own mother should have given her in the first place. This is also why some people have children; an unconscious attempt to get their emotional needs met in an unthreatening way. And so the cycle repeats.

Another reason people have children is to put right for

their children what was wrong with their own childhood. If a parent is desperate to make everything all right, or even as perfect as they can, for their child, they are not doing that for the child's benefit but rather to fulfil a need in themselves. Maybe they felt that their own childhood was a little bleak or cold or in some way lacking. A child is never 'spoilt' by too much love, but always by the wrong sort of love; in other words, love coming from the wrong place – the parent's unconscious need. This can be incredibly difficult to look at. So many people will say that of course they had a happy childhood even though they have very few memories of it. There is a guideline here that should always be applied: as humans we tend to forget sad times and remember the happy ones. If your childhood is a blank or a blur, be suspicious. An additional point to be wary of is the confusion between love and closeness. Many will claim closeness to their mother when, upon examination, it becomes clear that there was an enmeshed relationship dependent upon the mother's need masquerading as love. Children grow into adulthood with this mutual neediness still in place. Need is not love; nor is closeness automatically love, though the two may go hand in hand.

Hopefully by now, you are beginning to question what love is. It is not need and it is not necessarily closeness although it may encompass that. Love is unconditional acceptance of who the person is, not what they do; it has nothing to do with achievements or behaviour. And it is essential, whether your interaction is with a child or an adult, to always keep that distinction clear; "I love you but I do not like what you have just done."

People who have not been mirrored as babies have learnt that a mother's needs come first and hence, subsequently, everybody else's. This is justifiable cause for anger though; as children they will not have been allowed to express it and as adults may no longer recognise it. They may also have learnt that it is pointless asking for what they want because, at the very least, that request will be met with disapproval. Those needs do not go away and nor does the desire to have needs met, despite being buried under layers of denial, people-pleasing and over-adaptive behaviour. So, however many decades have passed, these people are still needy and have to find some way of getting their needs met. People will go to great lengths, unconsciously, to get themselves noticed in an attempt to continue receiving the negative attention they were used to as children; huffing and puffing, sighing, upsetting things or other people for, however fatuous, we are comfortable with what we are used to.

If we feel we are unable to ask for something directly, we default into a covert form of asking. This is manipulation and its purpose is to change someone else's behaviour, preferably without them realising. A request will be made in a devious way, probably in the guise of doing something for somebody else, certainly not for ourselves, and those on the receiving end of this behaviour will find that they are being manoeuvred into agreeing to something opposed to their original intentions. Help foisted upon one in these circumstances demands a high price in return because it is not done to satisfy the recipient but rather the needs of the giver who can then continue in the role of 'mummy's little helper'. It may not even be disguised as help. Perhaps someone wants a friend's advice but does not want to be seen to be asking, so a time to meet is arranged on the pretext of a mutual catch-up and the resulting conversation ends up being all about that person. If there is no awareness of what is happening, the first person will have got what he or she wanted without apparently asking, leaving the other potentially feeling used and resentful without understanding why. Both may vaguely recognise the fundamental dishonesty of the exchange.

Because these people habitually put others' needs and desires before their own, they are out of touch with what they want. Ask for an opinion and they have none. Ask them for a preference and they are stumped for an answer; they will always do what everyone else wants. When something goes wrong they will automatically assume the full burden of responsibility; it is their fault because it always has been. That was the price they apparently had to pay in order to keep their mothers happy. They are incapable of being true to themselves which has the unfortunate consequence of making them uncomfortable to be around.

These adults are not only out of touch with their needs

but also with their emotions. It is one of the greatest tragedies that our society belittles emotions in favour of the mental realm; both are equally important as attested to by anyone in a meaningful relationship. After all, relating is not primarily about thinking but about feeling. Denying our emotions is a very isolating experience and whilst this might arise from trauma, it is also likely to be a consequence of our early mothering. A baby's world, of which it is acutely aware, is one of feeling and sensation. Its inability, as yet, to verbalise experiences should not allow us to detract from them; however, a mother's inability to validate her child's emotion, does. The early experiences of a baby or small child are regularly dismissed on the grounds that they will not be remembered and that, therefore, they are unimportant. This erroneous assumption ignores many people's earliest body and emotional memories; the earlier the trauma, the deeper the scars, from birth and perhaps even pre-birth.

It is vital to validate all emotions. If a mother cannot bear to see her child cry, that child, in order to save its mother pain and to avoid incurring her disapproval, will repress its own expression of that pain; again, because its survival depends upon her. Perhaps nobody in a family ever expressed anger with the resultant message that anger is frowned upon, unsafe and disallowed. Or maybe, one person in that family was very angry and nobody else was allowed to be. Perhaps parents argued or constantly bickered, resulting in such an aversion that the child grew up determined never to be like them. Anger is probably the most disallowed emotion. We rarely experience it handled well and are not taught how to use it. Anger, like all emotions, has a valid role, but it must be expressed appropriately; that means to the right person, for the right reason, preferably at the right time and without bringing lots of previously unexpressed anger with it. As you become more emotionally aware and responsible, you will come to realise that rarely are we angry for the reason we think. Nobody has sufficient power over us to make us angry. However unreasonable and unattainable it sounds, we choose to feel what we feel. We often do not like it and that is a very good reason for doing our inner work; so that we can resolve issues that would otherwise cause us conflict and pain. Mostly when we are very angry, some unresolved problem from childhood has been triggered and it is then up to us to take some time out and trace it back to its origin. Too often, anger explodes violently because it has been repressed, sometimes for years.

Surprisingly, many people have problems with happiness. You might think that everybody wants to be happy and wants everybody else to be happy. Unfortunately this is often not so. Whilst they might not want to admit it, or even begin to understand it, a miserable parent can feel threatened or jealous of a happy child. In every family, each child assumes a particular role unconsciously approved of by that family: there might be the good, helpful child, the naughty child, the angry one and so on. But even in a mildly dysfunctional family there is no place for a happy child who is soon ground down. We also go along with the preconceived idea that all parents want their children to be successful: they often say so. Yet underlying that can be an unspoken, nevertheless clearly understood message, 'successful but not more successful than me/us'.

It is a mistake commonly made by parents to take no notice of their children when they are well-behaved. If the children are quietly playing, the mother can get on with household chores but if something goes wrong, her attention is needed. This is the beginning of the confusion between positive and negative attention. Children want, need and deserve positive attention, which, in addition to love and time, particularly requires genuine engaged communication. This means focussed eye contact, listening, mirroring and, above all, mental involvement. To be in a child's company, but to have your mind wandering or busy elsewhere, means you are physically present but emotionally absent and, therefore, putting your own needs before those of the child. If the adult is unable or unwilling to give positive attention, the child will demand negative attention because any attention is always better than none. In order to achieve this, the child will misbehave or have accidents; the more the parent over-reacts, the greater the reward for the child. A shouting mother or father is, at least, taking notice. It is, of course, the wrong sort of notice, a poor substitute for positive attention and therefore essentially unsatisfactory, which means that the child is in a cycle of demanding more and more. It is easy, then, to see how pity or anger becomes confused with love.

When pity is confused with love, people unconsciously want things to go wrong. This is very common and is frequently a component in health problems. A child may be ill to gain attention and to manipulate the parent's behaviour – "I can change your mind about sending me to school." An adult, deprived of attention throughout childhood, can guarantee sympathy and support when ill. This psychosomatic (the effect of the mind on the body) illness is not imagined or 'all in the mind'; it becomes a genuine physical illness originating in unresolved emotional (not mental!) issues. The good news is, of course, that if you can make yourself ill through what you feel or think, you may also enable your recovery through the same means. Victims abound and they thrive on drama. Some people's lives are awash with every conceivable trauma and they revel in it, drawing attention to themselves and talking of little else. Listeners collude by giving sympathy. We are brought up to believe that being sympathetic makes us nice, kind, caring people. It does nothing of the sort because it perpetuates and aggravates the problem. It is synonymous with jumping into a bog with a sinking victim instead of having the sense to help them get out. By giving them sympathy, we join in their negativity and we, ourselves, become negative. However, empathy enables us to stand strong and, from compassion, help the victim climb out to a place of strength and healing. Our so-called 'compensation culture' is the epitome of wanting things to go wrong, blaming someone else and not taking responsibility for ourselves.

Some parents are so fearful of losing their offspring's love that they indulge every childish whim and want to be their child's best friend. This always comes from the parent's need, however much they might try to persuade themselves otherwise. One of the ways children react to this is with sulky behaviour; they are angry that they are not receiving appropriate love yet not able to express this out of ignorance of the cause. And, of course, they do not want to lose the perceived benefits coming their way. Children who have not received even this distorted form of love are likely to be too withdrawn to manifest this sulkiness. This selfish parental behaviour effectually hands over to the child the power that should rightfully be the parent's. Children are naturally uncomfortable with this; knowing they are not yet mature enough to handle that power, they feel unsafe and realise that they cannot depend on their parents for the strength and boundaries that should be provided.

The power of projection

Unresolved emotional issues need to be drawn to our awareness in order that we can heal them. And one way this happens is through projection. From early childhood we have been forced into a position of denying many things about ourselves. Any behaviour, whether good or bad, that meets with disapproval is consigned to the 'shadow'. This is the dark unconscious and the more we practise denying anything about ourselves, the deeper it is driven into the shadow. We become so adept at this that if somebody was to confront us with something we have disowned, we would truly disbelieve them. We make the foolish assumption that if we cannot see it then neither will others. This denial in ourselves then makes itself known to us through seeing and strongly reacting to some trait or quality in another person. If, when we meet someone, we instantly strongly like or dislike something about them, we know that it is something unrecognised in us. And it then becomes our job to own it. Projection is constantly at work because we all have much about ourselves to integrate and because we live in a world of duality; right and wrong, male and female, us and them, so there is always someone else out there to carry for us that which we deem unacceptable in ourselves.

We also search out others to be the focus of our projection; like a hook on which to hang our problem. If we feel ourselves to have been rejected in childhood, out of familiarity with this pattern, we will perpetuate it with anyone subconsciously prepared to carry it for us despite any conflicting conscious desire for a close relationship. The same holds true of any other residual complex.

Inadequate parents (projecting their own inadequacies onto their children) control those children through fear, guilt and emotional blackmail. Each one of these can have devastating consequences for the future adult, leaving a legacy of anxiety and shame. For example: "Wait until you father comes home", "What will the neighbours say?", "What will people think of us if you...?", "Be quiet or you'll make your mother ill", "Don't upset your father".

A child requires love, positive attention and genuine, engaged communication. He or she also requires your behaviour to be consistent, never mind how tired or irritated you might be. When a child is thus valued and respected, he or she will automatically respect others. It is a sad reflection on society that we have lost respect for so much and that one of the things that adults and children alike are particularly sensitive about is respect or lack of it.

To be a parent and see in your children the consequences of your own unconscious beliefs and unresolved complexes can be shocking. To be aware of the pain you carry within yourself accrued as a result of your childhood experiences can be daunting indeed.

However, much of the damage can be repaired and that is what the next part of this book is about.

three

For the purposes of this book and of my work in general, I define 'inner child' as follows:

The concept of inner child

> The child that we were has been subjected to difficulties, emotional traumas and in some cases, a constant drip-feed of negative conditioning, the result being that we each have many different ages of traumatised or stuck children within us. These are our 'inner children'.

The logical mind will think so what? We can't change history. Many people will also say, "This is how I am. I can't change myself." What this means is that the person has never considered the possibility, doesn't know it's an option and certainly wouldn't know how to go about it. Others would not see the need for change assuming, in their ignorance, that they are quite happy; carrying all their burden of automatic reaction to situations, being weighed down by oppressive memories, and struggling to relate satisfactorily. Yet others would not want to change because they have manipulated those around them into fulfilling their needs for them. Sometimes, people who have come for therapy have told me that they had a wonderfully happy childhood, despite evidence to the contrary. Judicious questioning has revealed over-protective (needy) parents and a close (claustrophobic) relationship with them that the client has grown to resent.

No, we cannot change history but we can certainly change how we feel about it. That does not imply a mental discipline but rather an emotional transformation; a liberating journey that results in greatly improved relating and exponential happiness.

four

Whether or not you remember much of your childhood and whether those memories encompass highlighted incidents, constant background noise or pretty much nothing at all are, for the moment, unimportant. What we will be dealing with is emotion, even if it often passes unrecognised.

How to heal the inner child

As you proceed on this journey of finding your real self, you will become more aware of what you are feeling and you will also recover more memories. Some or many of these will be painful – that is why you repressed them in the first place. There is, after all, only so much that a small child can bear. We acquire defence mechanisms that enable us to cope in that moment; one of those being the ability to forget and to do this so profoundly that we would deny that those things ever happened to us. A child cannot hold two opposing beliefs simultaneously; if a parent was sometimes caring and at other times cruel, in the interests of its survival, the child will only remember the better times. People may spend the whole of their lives with only the comparatively good memories.

As memories resurface, it is helpful to remember that you are now an adult with the adult's ability to be detached; viewing what happened at one step removed. It can be helpful, too, to remind yourself that, whatever happened then, you survived. And if you survived then, you can now. And if you have got this far in wanting to heal yourself, you will! This emphasis on the adult rational mind can, at first, seem as though it is reinforcing the original denial of emotion, the fragmentation of the personality and hence the opposite of our goal of reintegration. However, the difference is between an unconscious split as happened in childhood and a temporary, conscious split, chosen by the adult in the interests of healing. We need to keep our adult and our inner child – at whatever age we are working with at that time – distinct and separate. The job of our adult part is to re-parent the child and we are unable to do that if we lose sight of either.

So, we work on the basis of being aware of our inner child and also the adult that we are. This serves another useful purpose in that, as we progress, we will uncover previously repressed emotion, some of which will be directed at our parents. As an adult, it is not appropriate for us to blame them and be angry with them; as a child, it is. By consciously keeping these two parts of ourselves separate, we can work with our inner child, allowing that part of us to feel and express its appropriate emotion whilst the adult part of us continues to have a reasonable on-going relationship with them. We never need to express directly this anger to our parents; this is our own inner, not outer, work though the results of this inner work will inevitably manifest themselves in our outer world. This can happen to such an extent that we end up having a hugely improved relationship with parents; more akin to equal adults than parent to child. Our rational mind may well tell us that we are wrong to feel anger at our parents, that we are being disloyal; after all, they did their best for us. We can justify their behaviour in all manner of ways; they had a very hard childhood, we feel sorry for them and so on. We are right to be understanding of this but, once again, we must make the distinction between thinking and feeling for none of that alters our own experience of childhood, and if our inner child felt angry, he or she was justified in so doing.

We must do for our inner child what any good parent automatically does, acknowledging and validating all emotions. The "I can see, hear or understand what you are feeling. In those circumstances, considering what was going on, you were right to feel that." But before we can undertake this vital step of mirroring, we need to establish communication with our inner child.

Imagination is one of the most powerful tools there is for it reaches directly into the unconscious; a picture truly is worth a thousand words. So, however 'weird', 'crazy' or 'foolish' this seems, remember that is because of our accustomed emphasis on the mind and thinking. Remember, too, that an emotional problem requires an emotional solution and that is what we are putting in place here. In this inner realm of feeling and imagination, intent is fundamental. What we so often fail to appreciate is just how powerful this is. We have a thought and the desire to implement it, we feel it and it is done.

Imagine that you are sending a message back to the 'little you' that was. You do not have to remember you at any particular age; intent is everything. And neither are we talking about seeing or hearing with our eyes or ears; we have inner senses that we can become aware of and perfect with use. When you first start doing this, you might think that you are 'making up' the responses, or indeed, the whole thing. Just go with it. It works. Rationalising is a defence against feeling: we do not have to explain everything in mental terms. An additional, though not essential aid in helping you access little you, is photographs of yourself as a child.

The message that you are sending to your inner child is firstly that you are there for them, that you have recognised the need for re-parenting and that you want to fulfil that role. This is like starting to open up the channel of communication and beginning to build up trust. This may take a little while to achieve or it may happen instantly. Whichever way it goes, suspend your critical mind. Trust is needed on both sides; from you, knowing that the process is happening and from your child who may be struggling to learn to trust an adult, perhaps for the first time.

Is there a child in your family or perhaps a friend's child to whom you have ever given truly focussed attention? If so, recall it so that you can replicate it for your own inner child. If not, think about what it means and how it might feel. Is there anyone who has ever, however fleetingly, given you this kind of focussed attention and how did it feel? If so, remember it and do it for yourself. If, as a child, you have never experienced this focussed attention, this 'nobody else in the whole world matters but you right now', then when you do first manage to replicate it, you will probably dissolve into tears. These are tears of recognition, joy, and relief and also of sadness that you never experienced this as a child; this profound acknowledgement that should be every child's birthright. If this is as far as you get for a while, then fine. This initial process alone is immensely healing.

Having established the line of communication, move on, when you are ready, to the acknowledgement and validation of specific emotion; the first of the vital three steps that you will be going through each time you work with your child. If, as an adult, you know that your prevailing mood is one of anxiety, go back to your child and feel into whether this relates to specific incidents or it was a permanent, all-pervasive state. What you say will vary accordingly. "I can see that you are always anxious and worried. That is totally understandable considering what was going on," – and here be specific, state the reason as you understand it – "Because your parents were always arguing," "Because you never knew what state your father would be in when he came home," "Because your mum was always depressed." In other words, you were right to feel what you felt; it was an entirely appropriate response. If the anxiety comes from one or more particular incidents, take your child back to them, one at a time and go through the same process. Again, it may take a little while before the child understands that you truly recognise what he or she is experiencing. The more you validate the emotional response, the stronger and healthier the child's sense of identity becomes. If you have never received this feedback and find that you are often unaware of what you are feeling, it is useful practice to acknowledge and validate your own current emotions. Pause, pay attention to your feelings, work out what they are then say to yourself, "I am feeling sad, angry" – whatever it is that you are feeling. "It's ok that I'm feeling that." "I give myself permission to feel that." We too often judge, criticise and condemn before we can fully recognise what we are feeling. We may have been ridiculed, belittled or humiliated for what we felt as children. And all this may have been done in the name of kindness by protective parents. "Let's make a joke out of this, you shouldn't feel that", is the subtext from parents who, themselves, cannot cope with the terror their child is feeling: to acknowledge that anguish is vital, however painful for the parent. Only then should the matter be made light of, if at all appropriate.

When working with baby you, it is important that

you remember to mirror the baby's facial expression. This crucial step for babies lets them know that you understand what they are feeling and that they are right to feel it: they then know that they are safe and secure. Of course you can also talk to little you as described above. However surprising it may seem, sometimes people need to do their inner work with the baby before it is even born. This can be incredibly effective because imagination and intent are such powerful tools.

How do you decide what age inner child to work with? The answer is that sometimes you do not; as you become more accustomed to doing this work, you will find that your inner child presents itself to you at an age appropriate for what you are working on. We all have a family of many inner children requiring our attention and sometimes we will be going from one to another.

At whatever age, they all require our love and that is what step two is all about; unconditional love and reassurance. "I'm here for you now." And please mean it and act on it; do not betray your inner child again as he or she was betrayed and let down before. This means regular contact and you sticking to your word. Honour agreements and if for some reason you are unable to, then apologise. Adult you is building trust with your inner child. And this brings us to the question of how often you should be looking in and doing this work. Especially to start with, little and often. At least once a day to establish rapport. As you become more familiar with this process, you might settle into a pattern of focussed attention and work once a day, but also find yourself carrying your child around with you and frequently acknowledging them. When everything is comparatively quiet with your inner work, you still need to be maintaining contact with your child. This is a very good time for quality attention; have fun with them, play together, enjoy yourselves. If you neglect your child during these peaceful times, you are doing to them what your parents did to you in that you are only giving attention when things go wrong: attention then becomes associated with negativity and pity. You will find that some problems respond so effectively to your work that you may never need to revisit them whilst others will require further application with attention being paid to different facets or different levels.

Your role is to be there for the child; to mirror, to be emotionally available and not be mentally distracted. Many children have had to fulfil their parents' needs from a very early age so you need to ensure that little you understands that this is not his or her purpose. It is never the job of the child to make it right for you the adult. They should not be put in a position of having to pick up on and then adapt to your mood in order to make you feel better. It is your job, temporarily, to put your own needs to one side and concentrate on mirroring your child.

It is vital for our self-esteem that we know that we are truly valued for who we are and not just for our achievements. We are accustomed to reserving our praise for attainments and successes. Give lots of positive feedback apart from this; children need to hear that they are loved and that they are special just for being who they are.

Step three concerns re-education. Your child now knows that you are there for him or her, that your love is unconditional and that you recognise and validate his or her emotions. But this is only a part of the task. Re-education is about dealing with the problem in a more constructive manner and also learning appropriate ways of channelling the emotions that have come up. If we take an example of a child who always feels lonely, step three is: "Because I am here for you, you no longer need to feel lonely."

Having allowed the expression of all the tears and the pain of the loss of what might have been – the essential mourning process – the child needs to understand the importance of moving on; of not perpetuating self-pity. This period of adjustment, of re-education, may take a while, not only for a child who has become accustomed to a victim role, but also for the parent who must learn not to tolerate such behaviour. It is very likely that the child is not only sad, but also angry because of the lack of attention from an, apparently uncaring parent. This anger needs expression: were it to be denied, it would lead to yet more suppression and potential future problems. Allowing and encouraging a child to shout and scream, safely expressing anger within a controlled environment is essential. Scribbling on large sheets of paper can be useful. Drawing a picture of the absent or abusive parent and then destroying the picture or throwing mud at it or repeatedly kicking it or jumping on it can be an invaluable means of channelling the anger at the person drawn. Sometimes, specific verbal retribution may be required. In imagination, an erring parent can be made to stand in front of the child and forced to listen, if necessary, with his or her mouth taped shut. If the child is small, imagine that he or she can stand on a chair, or that the adult has to sit on the floor. Give your child permission to express the outrage/he or she rightfully feels, about past abuse or neglect.

If the parent customarily refuses to listen, have the child shout through a megaphone. Of course we are 'only working with the imagination'. But you already know how powerful this is. What it means, too, is that we do not have the intent to hurt physically the perpetrator. This sort of exercise liberates the psyche and empowers the person. Relationships transform for the better because there are no longer years of denied anger bubbling away just below the surface looking for trouble.

A punchbag is wonderfully useful for older children and adults. You can enlist your child's help to draw a picture of the offending adult which then gets fastened onto the bag. With the intent that the child works through you, a lot of anger can be exorcised. Sometimes we do not know why we are angry, and, if feeling into the anger does not provide the reason, then sometimes violent physical activity will.

When emotions have been so painful that we have denied or not dealt with them, there is a natural, understandable reluctance to return to so much pain. We need not only to remember that we are now adults and, as previously mentioned, can therefore view these incidents from a different perspective but also that we can use techniques to help. One of these is to imagine that you are viewing events unfolding on a television screen; you are in control and can switch off, and on again, any time you choose. Little and often may be appropriate. Another is to imagine shrinking the size of the adult and increasing the size of the child. The adult may be tiny and only in monochrome whereas the child can be huge and in full colour. Although small children do not possess the necessary verbal skills, that should be no hindrance to your imagination allowing them to be able to express whatever sets the record straight and empowers them.

Whatever you do, do not fall into the comparison trap. This is where you decide that someone else's childhood has been more traumatic than yours and therefore you do not deserve to 'make a fuss' about what happened to you. This is a glorified defence mechanism that, given half a chance will stop you doing your work and sorting yourself out. It really is no concern of yours whether or not someone else's experiences were worse; what matters is that we each take responsibility for our own problems and sort them out.

Another frequently encountered problem is that this

is all too simple. As humans, we like and expect things to be complicated, to such a degree that we are suspicious of simplicity. The assumption is that if it is that easy, it couldn't possibly work. Or that if it was that simple, the person would have seen it all for themselves in the first place. I am, therefore insulting their intelligence or I am incredibly stupid in believing that it could possibly work. My defence is that over a lifetime's study and work I have witnessed the truly awe-inspiring results too many times to count. It has been a joy and a privilege to be able to aid that transformation. It is simple and it does work.

appendix one

These steps apply equally to bringing up a child and to healing your own inner child.

STEP 1   VALIDATION

Essential to acknowledge, respect and validate emotions of small child. Feelings are a child's life.

"I can see/hear/feel/understand that you are feeling sad/angry/hurt, etc. Under those circumstances you were right to feel that."

Mirroring of facial expression for babies.

Without validation you are doing again what was done to you.

STEP 2   LOVE

"I love you. You are wonderful, special and perfect just as you are without having to do anything to prove it. I am here for you, it is not your job to be here for me. Therefore you do not have to adapt to me or to be what you think I want you to be."

What every child should hear! It is not a child's responsibility to make it right for its parents.

STEP 3   RE-EDUCATION

We (adult me and little me) can now do things differently.

For example, "Because I am here for you and love you unconditionally, you no longer need to feel lonely." Or "I can see that you are very angry that Mum didn't take the time to listen and try to understand. What would you like to say to her?"

Without this step you perpetuate the victim mentality and do not resolve the problem.

appendix two

Examples

A *Male, late twenties, low self-esteem*

He had been an only child born to parents in a troubled marriage. The father was rarely there and his mother was depressed. She was always either crying or angry. All his early memories were of his appeals to his mother for attention being met with her ignoring him or her violence. He remembered crawling across the shiny floor to her, holding onto her leg and her kicking him away repeatedly. He remembered her shouting and screaming at him and him knowing that it was all his fault. When older, a plate of food would be slapped down in front of him with such force that the food ended up on the floor. He felt worthless. He was unable to keep a relationship with a girlfriend because as soon as they got close, he would be terrified that she would find out how worthless he was and he couldn't let that happen. He was in an uninspiring job that gave him no satisfaction.

His inner child work started with him, explaining to

little him that his mother's problems were her responsibility; that it was not his job to make it right for her. No child can ever 'make it right' for a parent.

Step 1

"I know, too, that you are feeling it's all your fault that Mum is so sad and angry and it seems like she doesn't love you. And the way she's behaving, it's understandable that you feel that."

Step 2

"But I tell you what, I'm here for you now. I love you. I'm going to give you all the attention you need."

Step 3

He imagined little him shouting at his mother, telling her not to be so selfish and to give him attention. He imagined punching her leg, the leg that had kicked him away. He cried a lot and found that expressing his feelings to his mother brought him much relief. Sometimes in his visualisation, she appeared not to hear and then he would get a megaphone and shout down it and make her listen to him. He knew that he could do all this safely because she, in his imagining, just had to take it all with no comeback.

As he began to feel more empowered, he was able to follow a similar process with his father and express his pain and sense of loss that his father had not been there for him. Later, that also turned to anger and the small child in him shouted and punched and kicked whilst the adult wrote lots of angry letters (never, of course, to be read by his father).

How you feel when, at some future date, you decide to destroy these letters will give you feedback concerning your progress. Should it be delight in the destruction, you will know that you still have unfinished business; alternatively, a genuinely neutral reaction is more likely to be indicative of resolution.

B Female, early forties. Relationship difficulties.

Found it difficult to talk to her husband. Felt 'claustro-phobic' around him. B was even beginning to wonder whether she should remain in the relationship because she was feeling so uncomfortable with him.

Smothering, controlling, needy mother who always knew what was best for her daughter. Father 'weak' always agreed with mother and gave in to her. Also a sister who had taken the 'easy way out' and always did what the mother wanted.

In therapy she began to realise that her mother's extreme neediness projected onto her as a child had resulted in adult her construing closeness as demands being made upon her about which she felt resentful. Forced, yet feeling unwilling to carry this burden as a child, she realised she was expe-riencing similar feelings around her husband as an adult.

She was beginning to have health problems and realised that she was using this as a means of escape both from her husband and mother and all her re-emerging emotions.

Step 1

"I can feel that you are upset and angry about your mum not being there for you. I know it feels like she doesn't love you for who you are and that's very sad. She always seems to be telling you what to do and doesn't listen to what you want."

Step 2

"I love you so much. I'm here for you and I'm listening to what you want."

Step 3

"Let's draw some pictures of how you feel. Let's draw a picture of mum and you can scribble all over it." And she watched in her mind's eye as little B did just that with huge enjoyment and then jumped up and down on the drawing.

By the time these steps had been repeated many times over, B was surprised and then delighted to realise how much better she was feeling around her husband. She was also beginning to put boundaries in place with her mother in that she was able to explain gently to her that she was now an adult and didn't need her mother to tell her what to do all the time.

C Male, fifties. Depression.

Father had died, mother still alive. Although married, he spent a lot of his time with his mother looking after her. He had two brothers, one three years younger, one five years younger. Had a 'happy childhood'. Except on questioning, it turned out that he hadn't. As the eldest, he had been put in charge of his brothers and was punished if they got hurt or got into trouble, which happened often. He spent a lot of time justifying his mother's behaviour along the lines of her tough childhood and his father rarely being at home. When father was there, he was 'always walking away'. If his son was good and quiet, the father wasn't needed and so walked away. If he was naughty, Father still walked away and left the discipline up to Mother. It seemed as if there was nothing that he could do to get his father's attention, never mind his approval.

As we began to explore these issues, C started to get in touch with anger. At first he was very uncomfortable with this, feeling he was being disloyal to his parents. The further we progressed with inner child work, making the distinction between his childhood anger, which had had no place to go, and his rational adult self, the better he became. He discovered the direct correlation between his previously denied anger and his depression: the more he expressed his anger, the less the depression.

Step 1

"It's all right that you're angry with Mum. You should never have been made responsible for your little brothers."

"It's all right that you are angry with Dad. He never really was a dad was he? He never gave you time, attention or anything at all. You're right to be angry that he was always walking away."

Step 2

"But I'm here for you now and I'm going to be a good parent, like a wonderful mum and dad all in one."

Step 3

Socially acceptable expression of anger. Punchbag was invaluable. He was able to imagine the little boy he had been, there with him, punching out his rage at his parents.

D Female, early twenties. Career guidance.

She had various ideas but felt unable to act upon them. Her parents were encouraging and assured her that they would support whatever decision she arrived at. She still lived at home with them.

Although she came wanting career advice, that was not the problem. It was her inability to be responsible for herself. She excused her lack of decision-making as 'perhaps it would be the wrong one'.

I always ask people what they know concerning their birth. As I've already mentioned, early problems can leave profound difficulties and that was so here. Her birth had been induced and it had been a lengthy labour. When she felt back into this situation, she said she had the distinct impression that she had not been ready to be born and that the midwife delivering her had forced her to do something against her wishes.

To many people, this may sound incredible: perhaps even unbelievable. But in my experience, I have come across a number of similar situations. Even though our mind may not remember, our bodies certainly do and emotions replay themselves until addressed.

She needed to work with the anger she felt at the midwife for apparently forcing her to be born and she needed to reclaim her life and decisions; to know that they were not in someone else's hands (literally). She also needed to overcome the resistance that she had used as a form of rebellion against what was being done to her at the time of her birth.

STEP 1, 2 AND 3

She visualised herself just before being born and really listened to what little her was feeling. This turned out to be a lot of fear.

"I can feel your fear. It's all right that you're frightened, but I am here for you now and I'll stay with you. I know you are frightened of this birth and worried that you might not survive but I know that you did survive because I'm here now." (Three steps in one here.)

Once she had reassured baby her, she was able to move on to working with her anger at the midwife.

STEP 1

She looked again at baby her and reflected back to her the furious expression. "It's so understandable that you feel angry with the midwife when you didn't want to be born then." And she gave baby her permission to scream and shout at the midwife, telling her that she didn't want to be born and to leave her alone.

STEP 2

She 'saw' herself holding baby her, mirroring the facial expression and telling the baby how much she loved her.

STEP 3

Having visualised herself being safely born, as indeed she had been, she set about explaining that because the birth had been safe and gone well, she could now start to feel happy about being born then. There was no longer a need to resist or rebel. She explained, too, that as she grew up, she would like to be able to make decisions of her own accord. No longer did she need to feel that decisions were forced upon her.

E Female, late thirties. Lack of relationship.

She had been adopted when just a few days old by a couple whose dysfunctional marriage added to her problems. Her depressed (angry) mother and overtly angry father had, I suspected, prejudiced her against relationships. She was lacking in self-confidence and generally unhappy.

STEP 1

"I know that you feel unwanted because you birth mother gave you away. I know that you feel you were not good enough and that's why she gave you away."

STEP 2

"But I am here for you now and I love you so much that it is more than going to make up for that." I advise clients to feel love really flowing from their heart into their little child and E did this most successfully. Many years of repressed pain and tears came flooding out, and she took a while to integrate all this before moving on to the next step.

She spent a long time giving baby and little her lots of love, acceptance and appreciation just for being who she was. E followed this up with teenager work; the girl she had been had felt isolated, unaccepted, unacknowledged and worthless. As a result, her early experience of boyfriends had not been good. As she had grown older, her adopted father's behaviour towards her had become more vitriolic and the parents' difficulties more acute.

STEP 3

She explained to different ages of her that things could be very different. Fortunately she had friends whose parents were much healthier role models, and she was able to use this as a starting point for the understanding that good relationships could happen for her, not just other people. She made a composite of these parents, taking from each the qualities that she would have most desired in ideal parents. She ended up with imaginary 'ideal' parents on loan for a while to help her heal. Both of these 'perfect' parents were always there for her in the right way. They were loving, accepting and valued her enormously.

As her own appreciation of herself increased, so she found that others appreciated her more and the story had a happy ending. Because of the work she had done on herself, she had a happy marriage and two delightful children to whom she was a really good mother.

F Female, forties. Anxiety.

A friend suggested she come although F did not understand the need for the visit. Didn't really have any problems except anxiety which she had always had. A sort of low grade general unease. Looked at other people's lives and saw how many of them had major difficulties. Thought she ought to feel lucky. In a happy marriage to a successful businessman. Had two adult children.

She had a brother, four years younger, who was totally adored by their mother when they were children. Her father loved her and gave her attention. But this turned out to be when she had done well in school or when she danced for him. As a child, dancing had become her life, something in which she could totally immerse herself and escape, and deny her understandable jealousy of her brother.

Step 1

It took a long time for F to begin to make contact with little her. Eventually she was able to ask her inner child what she was feeling. Again, a lengthy silence. She had had so much practice at cutting off from her feelings that it took a while for her to get back in touch. She began to realise how unappreciated she had felt. Her brother had always been the centre of attention and it had felt as though 'there was no room' for her. So, she mirrored this back to her inner child. "I can see that you feel unhappy and lonely and most of all not really loved. It's all right that you feel jealous and resentful of your brother when he seemed to be getting all the love." Overcoming years of denial and repression was a very big step for her, so it was important that she frequently praised little her and continued to give her permission to go on exploring her emotions.

She realised that she had only received attention for achievements, not for who she was. "I'm here for you now. I love you and know you are special and wonderful just for being who you are. You don't have to do anything to prove it."

Step 3

"Your parents loved you though they were not able to show it in the way you needed and every child has a right to." F carried her inner child around with her and constantly gave her the approval she had craved, repeating Step 2 many times over. She also reached a point where she was able to acknowledge to herself her anger with her mother and to work with it. This greatly improved their relationship because F was no longer unconsciously projecting anger onto her mother whenever they met.

G Female, fifties. 'Lonely' and ill.

Had been ill 'most of her life'. Actually remembered in her twenties wanting to be ill and trying to make herself ill. A child born to a depressed mother and absent father, she had been starved of affection all her life. Married to a businessman who was always away, mostly abroad. Said she was desperately lonely.

I started by explaining the difference between alone,

meaning on her own, and lonely, more a self-pitying state of mind about being on one's own. And the fact that we all have a choice about what we feel. This was difficult for her; she couldn't believe that she 'chose' to feel lonely although, as I reminded her, she had told me about her choice to be ill. As we talked, it became obvious that she used illness as an attempt to get attention. I explained about some people confusing love with pity and how this cycle of negative attention led to, amongst other things, illness. We had to take this all very slowly for she was reluctant to change, fearing for how her life might be were she to do so.

Eventually, she started doing some inner child work. She found the preparatory stage of communication with little her devastating. She found the loneliness, pain and neglect almost incomprehensible. She kept asking, "How could someone do that to a child?" She finally managed to acknowledge and validate the feelings of the child she had been. G had connected so effectively with her inner child that it was then easy for her to give her child lots of love and attention in a positive way. And by then, she understood that she did not need to be ill in order to get that attention.

H Male, late thirties. Concerned about his drinking.

Born third in a family of five children. 'Lost in the middle somewhere.' A happy childhood in that the children, who were all close in age, played together and appeared to be united against their common foe – their parents. Parents stressed out, both working hard, too tired to spend time with their children. Not much money, clothes handed down and a general feeling of lack about everything. Mother had died when H was in his early teens and the children had had to fend for themselves. 'Nothing different there then.'

Step 1

A lonely, lost little boy pretending he was all right, craving adult attention. Acknowledging and validating his childhood emotions brought so many realisations about the emptiness of his life and how he had tried to fill it with so many inappropriate things, not least, alcohol. "I can see that you don't think you're lonely because you have your brothers and sister, but I know that underneath that you are feeling lonely and that's understandable because neither of your parents was there for you in any way."

Step 2

"I can see that you really need lots of love and that's what I'm going to give you."

Although the adult part of him understood why his parents had behaved the way they had and that they were misguided, the child part of him was ready to express his rage at their absence. He let this happen. He would run and stamp out his anger letting the little boy he had been do this through him. The adult part of him wrote them letters – the sort you always keep to yourself – explaining how he felt they had neglected and abandoned him.

He soon reached a point of being able to deal with his emotions without trying to block them out or running away from them. And then he was able to enjoy a drink socially.

I Female, late twenties. Anxiety.

Had a younger brother who she constantly tried to protect throughout childhood. He had asthma and would react badly every time their mother left or threatened to, which was frequently.

STEP 1

She explained to little her that it was so understandable that she had felt responsible for her brother but that it never should have been her responsibility. She acknowledged and validated her inner child's anger with her mother for her irresponsibility and her frequent departures. She also acknowledged her anger with her father for not stopping her mother. And then she realised how helpless little her had felt.

Step 2

Lots of acceptance, love and appreciation for little her. "I love you. You were amazing to cope with what you did and to help your brother so much. But now you don't have to do any of that. I love you just for who you are."

Step 3

Channelling the anger: little her imagining tying up her mother so that she could not leave, beating her, screaming at her and demanding that she look after her two children properly. There were lots of tears and lots of emptiness to be worked on.

J Female, seventies. 'Unhappy'.

"My daughters used to love me but now they avoid me. They used to do so much for me. Not any more, they're always so busy. I can't think what's come over them," and so on. By the time she eventually finished complaining, I was beginning to wonder if her daughters had a point.

She was born the eldest of six and was responsible for bringing up the whole family from the age of seven when her mother had died, giving birth to the youngest. This was during the Second World War and would have been an achievement for an adult, never mind a child of her age. One of the consequences of this was that because all her time was taken up looking after her younger siblings, she never got her own needs met; she could never ask for what she wanted. She did not know how and there would have been no point in her trying. As an adult, she continued this pattern of behaviour, looking after her sick husband and trying to do the same for her daughters who, as they grew up, distanced themselves from her in protest.

It was a struggle to get J to understand that it was all right for her to know what she wanted and once that was achieved, she struggled, again, with the concept that she could ask directly for something. This was the crux of the problem for it was her roundabout way of trying to get somebody to do something for her (manipulation) that had caused her daughters such a problem. She would start off a conversation complaining about something – with the intention of getting someone to feel sorry for her – whereupon they would rush to help. She had trained her daughters to 'save' her and now they were rebelling.

STEP 1

She could remember no experience of being mothered and had little experience of mothering in a positive way. She was unable to think of anyone she knew who was an ideal mother figure so, in her case, we worked together to make up the perfect mother. It was only when we had introduced this imaginary, but most important, figure to little J that she was able to start effectively with her inner child work. This imaginary mother showed her what she needed and the blocks and defences began falling away. Then J was able to take over responsibility and mirror back to little her the desperate emptiness.

This was only possible having first used the imaginary mother figure. Then adult J could say to little her, "I'm here for you. I love you. It's all right for you to ask me for what you want."

With lots of practice, this became easier and over a period of time, her daughters noticed a difference and they were able to begin rebuilding their relationship.

This use of an "Imaginary Mother" can be beneficial for anyone who has, for whatever reason, lacked the experience of being mothered, particularly as a baby. She is to represent all the qualities and characteristics you would wish for in an ideal mother. These can be attributes you have seen in other mothers or purely imagined on your part. She is to be the epitome of mirroring, loving and nurturing. Once you have established your connection and ongoing visualisation, you as an adult can then take on the responsibility of good parenting – the three steps. This is essential, for tempting as it might appear to bask in the comfort and security of this mother's love, this would eventually impede your continued progress.

Similarly, some people go straight to step 2 and stay there because it is easy, enjoyable and perhaps also because it reflects their childhood when they were never "mirrored": the tendency is to keep reassuring the inner child with such platitudes as "It is all right", "It will be all right". This is both misleading and dishonest. It reinforces the childhood damage and is no preparation for how to handle future challenges. Children are incredibly intuitive and pick up on anxieties, fears, etc.; they fully realise if someone is saying one thing and meaning another. What this does is to confirm their lack of trust. Surely, correct mirroring is preferable: "You look worried, that's understandable, I am worried, too, but I am the adult here and I'm going to find a way to deal with this."

You may need to revisit your inner child from time to time even when you think the basic groundwork is complete. For example, when some difficulty arises in your adult life, it is to be expected that your emotional reaction goes back to childhood: work through that and you can then respond as a rational adult. Additionally, you may find it useful to re-parent adult you, at whatever age, using the same three steps as guidelines.

Lightning Source UK Ltd.
Milton Keynes UK
UKHW021223210319
339599UK00010B/527/P